The City

by Emily C. Dawson

amicus readers

1

Amicus Readers are published by Amicus
P.O. Box 1329, Mankato, Minnesota 56002

Printed in the United States of America at Corporate Graphics, North Mankato,
Minnesota.

Library of Congress Cataloging-in-Publication Data
Dawson, Emily C.
  The city / by Emily C. Dawson.
     p. cm. -- (Amicus readers. My community)
  Includes bibliographical references and index.
  Summary: "Describes a trip to the city and typical things one might do when
visiting a large city. Includes visual literacy activity"--Provided by publisher.
  ISBN 978-1-60753-022-0 (library binding)
  1. Cities and towns--Juvenile literature. 2. City and town life--Juvenile
literature. I. Title.
  HT152.D38 2011
  307.76--dc22
                          2010011119

Editorial Credits
Series Editor   Rebecca Glaser
Series Designer   Mary Herrmann
Book Designer   Bobbi J. Wyss
Photo Researcher   Heather Dreisbach

Photo Credits
Alex Segre/Alamy, 13, 20 (t); Andre Jenny/Alamy, 15, 20 (b); John Kelly/Getty
Images, 17; Juan Luis Jones Herrera/iStockphoto, multiple pages (watermark);
Patti McConville/Alamy, cover; Philip Scalia/Alamy, 5, 20 (m), 21 (t); Pioneer
Court House Square, 1, 7, 21 (b); travelstock44/Alamy, 11, 21 (m); Wang Leng/
Getty Images, 9

1223
42010

10 9 8 7 6 5 4 3 2 1

Contents

Let's visit the city and go downtown. We'll ride the light rail train to get there.

downtown

light rail train

We get off the train and walk across the town square. Flowers are on display for a garden festival.

town square

The gift shop downtown has scarves on sale. We buy a pretty scarf for Aunt Sara's birthday.

We see our friend Laila and her sister at the museum. They are looking at a display of native art.

museum

11

We stop to eat lunch at a café. The special is potato soup. The café is busy so we sit outside.

café

Then we walk to the harbor. We watch the boats coming in to dock.

harbor

Our friend Ben is at the park. We run to play with him on the monkey bars. Then it's time to go home.

What a busy day in the city! Can you spot all the places we went on the map?

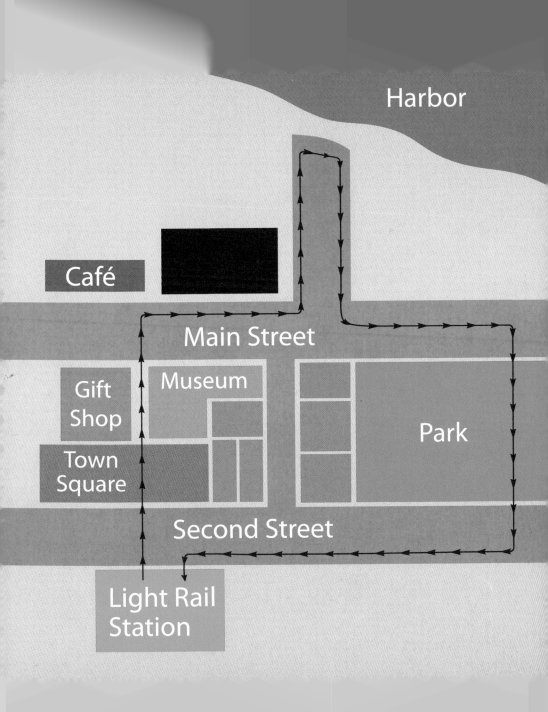

Harbor

Café

Main Street

Gift
Shop

Museum

Park

Town
Square

Second Street

Light Rail
Station

Picture Glossary

café—a small restaurant

downtown—a city's main business area, with stores, offices, restaurants, and places to visit

harbor—a place where boats are kept when not in use

light rail train—a train that takes people into and around cities

museum—a place where interesting objects of art, history, or science are displayed

town square—a large open area where people can gather for events

City Puzzler: A Second Look

Take a second look at the photos and map in the book to answer these questions.

1. What building is across from the cafe?

2. Where is there an American flag?

3. What season is it?

Check your answers on page 24.

Notes for Parents and Teachers

My Community, an Amicus Readers Level 1 series, provides essential support for new readers while exploring children's first frame of reference, the community. Photo labels and a picture glossary help readers connect words and images. The activity page teaches visual literacy and critical thinking skills. Use the following strategies to engage your children or students.

Before Reading
- Ask the students to tell you what they know about cities.
- Look at the cover and title page photos. Ask students to describe what they see.
- Show students the table of contents.

While Reading
- Read the book aloud, or have the students read independently.
- Point out the photo labels. Show students how to refer to the picture glossary for more information.

After Reading
- Invite the students to return to the book and talk about the sequence of the narrator's trip to the city. Prompt them with questions, such as, *Where did they go first? Where did they go after that?*
- Ask the students to look at the map on page 18 to check if their sequence was correct.
- Have the students think about a city they have visited. Ask them where they went. How was their trip similar to or different from the one in the book?

INDEX

WEB SITES

Constitutional Walking Tour of Philadelphia
http://www.theconstitutional.com/tour.php

Downtown Los Angeles Walking Tour
http://college.usc.edu/geography/la_walking_tour/

Safe Walking for Kids
http://www.nysgtsc.state.ny.us/Kids/kidswalk.htm

ANSWERS FROM PAGE 22

1. The gift shop

2. On a domed building behind the town square

3. Summer